GW00393415

FASCINATING FACTS
about
IRELAND

Michael Smith

Illustrated by
Nick Scott

WHITE ROW

The White Row Press

FASCINATING FACTS
about
IRELAND

Michael Smith

Illustrated by
Nick Scott

WHITE ROW

The White Row Press

First published 1993
by the White Row Press
135 Cumberland Road, Dundonald
Belfast BT16 OBB

Text copyright © Michael Smith
Illustrations copyright © Nick Scott
All rights reserved

Cover: detail from September Evening, Ballymote,
by Colin Middleton (Ulster Museum, Belfast), reproduced
with the kind permission of Mrs Kate Middleton.

Typesetting: Island Publications
Printed by the Guernsey Press Company Limited

A catalogue record for this book is available
from the British Library

ISBN 1 870132 65 3

Contents

Michael Smith was born in 1966, and moved to Fermanagh at the age of eleven. His spectacularly unsuccessful educational career culminated in a year at the University of Wales, which was spent, instead, in London and Amsterdam. His working life since has included stints as a plasterer, hotel porter, sometime journalist, and tailor. His ambition is to direct a remake of the classic movie Odd Man Out.

Nick Scott is a musician and graphic artist, who is much too modest to have his biographical details recorded. He lives in Belfast.

Preface

THE island of Ireland, lying on the edge of the known world for most of recorded history, has long excited the imagination of observers.

Ptolemy believed Hibernia to be a land permanently covered by fog and inhabited by man-eating giants. In the 12th century, the Norman-Welsh chronicler Giraldus Cambrensis wrote of a country with islands where people could live forever, and on which no woman could set foot and live. In 1572, the Englishman Edmund Campion, sent as a spy by Elizabeth I, returned from Ireland with a report full of so many oddities that it ultimately cost him his head. In the 19th century, folklorists uncovered a whole new layer of local tradition, custom and legend, which was every bit as extraordinary as the fictions of the early observers.

This book also delves into the extraordinary, chronicling nearly three hundred arcane, and I hope, interesting and amusing facts and brief

anecdotes, relating to Ireland and its people.
Law and Disorder tracks down the crooks and
con-men who have either disgraced or delighted
Ireland down through the centuries, and, in so
doing, comes across a novel medieval method of
settling one's income tax difficulties. *City Streets
and Countrysides* offers a breakneck tour of some
of the more obscure aspects of the country's
topography. In *Saints and Scholars*, a look at the
idiosyncrasies and achievements of the holy,
you will find the connection between Lough
Derg and Hell. *Eerie Eire* tells of the County
Down beauty spot which stubbornly defies the
laws of gravity. *Arms and the Man* is all about
that favourite Irish occupation, fighting, and
recounts the strange saga of the 18th century
battle in Italy between the French and Austrians
that ended in a stunning Irish victory. *Not a lot
of people know that...* ties up the loose ends, and,
amongst other things, recalls the Kerry town
that found it quicker to get its post from New
York than Dublin.

Most of the material has been mined from
local histories, newspapers, guides and the
ancient legends of Ireland, gathered over years
of casual collecting. The following, however,
have proved valuable works of reference and
deserve special mention: Adrian McLoughlin's
City of Belfast, and *The Streets of Ireland*, Peter
Somerville Large's *Dublin*, and *Irish Eccentrics*,
Ida Grehan's *Irish Family Names*, Julia and Brian

O'Shea's *Guide to Irish London*, Peter Bowler and Jonathon Green's *What a Way to Go*, Patrick Montague's *Saints and Martyrs of Ireland*, Adrian McLoughlin's *Guide to Historic Dublin*, Sean Jennett's *The West of Ireland*, John Watney's *Travelscapes Ireland*, Catlan Younger's *Ireland's Civil War*, and *The Guinness Book of Records*.

I will leave you with a quote from that legendary wit, Oscar Wilde:

> There is only one thing worse than being talked about and that is not being talked about

a fate which, for better or worse, will never befall either Ireland or its people.

Michael Smith
Lisnaskea

LAW AND DISORDER

ARGUABLY the oddest criminal in history was 'Billy the Bowl', who terrorised the streets of 18th century Dublin. Born without legs, Billy moved around in an iron bowl specially made for him by a sympathetic blacksmith. Tiring of begging for a living, Billy turned to robbery and murder before his arrest and execution in 1786.

THE police station in Dungannon, County Tyrone, should overlook the Khyber Pass. In the 19th century, the plans for this fearsome fortress-type building were sent by mistake to Ireland instead of India.

IN Sligo, you still officially need a licence to buy molasses – a legal hangover from the days when the county was the poitin capital of Ireland.

DURING the 1920s, when the electric railway opened between Portrush and Portstewart, crafty farmers were quick to spot an opportunity for profit. They would leave the carcasses of dead cattle by the line and then claim compensation from the railway company for the electrocution of their animals.

IN 1973, IRA chief of staff Joe Twomey made a spectacular escape by helicopter from Dublin's Mountjoy Prison. In the confusion, the guards made a vain attempt to thwart his plan by shutting the prison gates.

IN 1610, the town council of Youghal, County Cork, became so concerned about 'divers lewd persons' deflowering virgins that they passed a law against them. Fines ranged from £40 if the girl was the daughter of an alderman, down to £5 if she was only the offspring of a groom.

DURING the bitter Act of Union debate of 1800, the Irish parliamentarian Buck Whaley voted twice, once for the motion and once against, and, in the process, picked up a bribe from both camps.

THE last survivor of the infamous 1789 mutiny on *The Bounty* was John Adams from Derry.

IN 1980, an anonymous Tyrone alcoholic met a dreadful death. Taking a sip from a lemonade bottle he assumed contained poitin, he found to

In 1671 the British Crown Jewels were stolen by an Irish adventurer Colonel Thomas Blood, who was arrested soon after in a tavern while trying to barter one of the precious jewels for ale. Charles II was so impressed that he gave Blood a full pardon, and rewarded him with an estate in Ireland.

*One in three of Ireland's gaming machines is in the
seaside resort of Bundoran, County Donegal.*

his horror that the clear liquid was sulphuric acid – he died in agony several hours later.

IRISHMAN Michael Barrett holds the dubious distinction of being the last person to be publicly executed in the British Isles. He was wrongly hanged for the Clerkenwell bombing of 1867.

AFTER his execution in 1830, the skin of the Cork-born bodysnatcher William Burke was cut up and made into snuff pouches and wallets.

DUBLIN'S Nelson's Pillar (blown up by the IRA in 1966) was built before Nelson's Column in London.

THE Rotterdam Bar in Belfast's docklands was once a prison for convicts awaiting transportation to Australia.

SHOT dead in 1513, Garrett Mor Fitzgerald, Earl of Kildare, is the first recorded victim of the gun in Ireland.

IN 1992, Fermanagh solicitor Terence Gibson appeared in Enniskillen Crown Court representing the man who had crashed into his car. His defence was unsuccessful and his client was ordered to pay Mr Gibson £130 in damages.

DEATH by hanging is still on the statute book

in the Republic of Ireland. Although it is
sometimes given, the sentence is always
commuted. However, the gallows at Mountjoy
Prison are still kept in working order. Just in
case...

IRISH petty criminal J. P. Hannan escaped from
Verne Prison in Dorset, England, in 1955 just
one month into a 21 month sentence. He is still
at large.

IT was a crime in medieval Waterford to refer to
someone as 'an Irishman'.

THE mob which stormed the Bastille in 1789,
thus sparking off the French Revolution,
included Joseph Kavanagh, a cobbler and *agent
provocateur* from County Clare.

IRISHWOMAN Mary Kelly was the last victim
of Jack the Ripper in 1888. It was her liver that
the killer posted to Scotland Yard.

LIZ McClelland died in Christchurch, New
Zealand, in 1972 at the age of 80 after she was
struck on the head by a placard during a pro-
IRA march she had got caught up in while out
shopping. Just two years before, she had
emigrated from her native Belfast 'to get away
from the violence'.

Resurrection Men were graverobbers who operated in 18th century Ulster. Stealing fresh bodies from cemeteries, they would put the cadavers in barrels of whiskey to preserve them for the voyage to Scotland, where doctors dissected them in the name of science.

In Mid-Ulster, at the turn of the century, local peasants drank ether, which produces a sensation similar to LSD.

DURING an outbreak of agrarian violence in 1820, the highly unpopular Richard Long, landlord of Longfield in County Tipperary , was shot dead while sitting on the toilet.

EVERY Irish monastery that was sacked by the Vikings was also raided – at least once – by Irish lords.

LYNCHING originated with Galwayman Colonel Charles Lynch, who, during the American War of Independence (1775-1783), hanged without trial any British redcoats unfortunate enough to fall into his hands.

THE great Ulster chieftain Shane O'Neill once reportedly cut off the ears of a servant who was late with his supper.

IN 1586, the Bishop of Ossory, Nicholas Walsh, was stabbed to death in the pulpit during mass by a man he had just publicly denounced for adultery.

FOUNDED in 1814 by Rir Robert Peel, the Royal Irish Constabulary was the world's first organised police force.

IN 1792, inspired by the events of the French Revolution, pupils at Belfast Royal Academy mutinied and seized the school building. After unsuccessfully trying to shoot their headmaster, they surrendered quietly to the militia.

THE Shakespearean villain Richard III is said to be based on the 16th century rebel, Gerald, Earl of Desmond.

DURING a celebrated murder trial in 18th century Dublin, the powerful Santry family threatened to cut off the city's water supply (which ran through their estate) unless their son was cleared of all charges. The jury returned a unanimous verdict of 'not guilty'.

BELFAST'S first sectarian riot took place in 1832.

CASTLEBAR, County Mayo, is owned by the runaway Lord Lucan, who vanished in 1974.

IN 1734, students at the then notably lawless Trinity College murdered an unpopular dean by the name of Edward Forde.

STRONGBOW, the Norman conqueror of Leinster, is said to have cut his young son in two with one stroke of his broadsword because the frightened child showed cowardice. This appalling story is given credence by, or perhaps originates in the fact that the effigy of the upper

The medieval O'Flaherty clan of Galway had a novel method of dealing with tax collectors. Inviting the unsuspecting official to dine with them, they made sure to sit him at the head of the table in the place of honour. At the pull of a hidden lever, the floor would open up beneath their victim plunging him to his death in a deep well below.

In medieval Dublin, any woman found crying out after dark without good reason had to forfeit all her clothes on the spot.

half of a small boy lies beside his tomb in Dublin's Christchurch Cathedral.

THE famous Irish-American boxer 'Gentleman' Jim Corbett had a particularly effective knockout punch – before a fight he would soak the bandages wrapped round his fist in Plaster of Paris.

THE grandmother of the famous revolutionary, Che Guevara, was from Galway.

THE notorious 18th century Dublin hellraiser Buck English once shot a waiter dead and then had his victim added to the bill for £50.

IN ancient Ireland, a man who was not whole could not be leader of a *tuath* or kingdom. Losers in succession feuds often had their eyes gouged out by the victor.

CITY STREETS, COUNTRYSIDES

THE original Abbey Theatre in Dublin was opened in 1904 on the site of a morgue.

IVAN Beshoff, the former owner of Beshoff's fish and chip shop in Dublin, was the last survivor of the famous 1905 mutiny on the battleship *Potemkin*. He died in 1987 aged 104.

DESPITE the fact that the border has been in place for more than seventy years, the waters of Carlingford Lough are still in dispute between the United Kingdom and the Republic of Ireland.

THERE is a Donegal woven carpet weighing five tons in the Grand Foyer of Belfast City Hall.

ST. James's Gate Brewery is built on the site where, since medieval times, Dubliners held an

*The world's most northerly vineyard is
in Mallow, County Cork.*

The prehistoric tombs at Newgrange in County Meath are older than the Great Pyramids of Egypt.

annual drinking festival every 25th July to celebrate the feastday of St. James.

FOR many years, the headquarters of Sinn Fein and the Orange Order were next door to each other at numbers 9 and 10 Parnell Square, Dublin.

NEW York's Central Park was modelled on St. Stephen's Green.

EUROPE'S highest cliffs are on Achill Island, off County Mayo. Dropping over 2000 feet into the Atlantic Ocean, they are nearly twice the height of the world's tallest building.

BALBRIGGAN, County Dublin, was once the hosiery capital of the world. Around the turn of the century stockings and tights were widely known as 'Balbriggans'.

THE sinister sounding Bloody Foreland in County Donegal owes its name to its magnificent sunsets.

COVERING some 400 square miles, the midland Bog of Allen is the largest peat bog in the world.

THE lunar-like landscape of the Burren in County Clare is the only place in the world where arctic and sub-tropical flora grow side by side.

THE largest carillon of bells in the British Isles (128 of them) is housed in the spire of St. Colman's Cathedral in Cork.

THE eastern profile of the Cave Hill, which dominates the Belfast skyline, is known as 'Napoleon's Nose' because of its likeness to the profile of the famous French emperor.

IRELAND'S largest 'Chinatown', with a community 5,000 strong, is in the Botanic area of Belfast.

THE wealthy New York resort of Coney Island is named after a small uninhabited island off the coast of County Sligo.

IRELAND'S only gold rush took place in 1795 at Croghan in the Wicklow Mountains. It made no-one rich.

VENTRY, in County Kerry, was founded by an evangelical society as a home for converts from catholicism.

THE parlous state of the Irish economy during the 1980s may perhaps be explained by the fact that a favourite meeting place of the country's

*At its narrowest point, the North Channel
separates Ireland from Scotland by a
mere eight miles.*

During a raging storm in 1639, the kitchens of Dunluce Castle on the Antrim coast collapsed into the sea, taking with them all but one of the servants who were busily preparing a grand feast.

top economists was then Doheny and Nesbitt's bar in Dublin.

YOU can only call yourself a true Dubliner if you were born between the North and South Circular Roads.

EVERY spring, more than twenty million eels swim into the River Bann to breed.

EMMET Square in Birr, County Offaly, marks the centre of Ireland.

FIVEMILETOWN in County Tyrone is more than six miles from the nearest village. The measures that named it were the longer 'Irish' miles.

THE Giant's Causeway contains over 40,000 basalt columns.

DUBLIN'S Ha'Penny Bridge is so called because that was the original toll required to cross it.

ST. Columb's Cathedral in Derry was the first Cathedral to be built after the Reformation.

THE Guinness-owned St. James's Gate Brewery in Dublin covers 60 acres. It is the biggest in the world.

MULGRAVE Street in Limerick, which contains two hospitals, a prison and a lunatic asylum, is known as 'Calamity Avenue' by the locals.

THE Nephin Beg, a 200 square mile wilderness in County Mayo, is the only part of the Irish mainland to be completely uninhabited.

THE only nudist beach in Ireland is at the Forty Foot Leap, by the Sandycove martello tower, in Dun Laoghaire.

LOUGH Erne is said to have an island for every day of the year – in fact, it only has 154.

OXMANTOWN in Dublin, part of the site of the old Viking city, has one of the highest concentrations of blondes in Ireland.

THE curiously named town of Hospital in County Limerick owes its name to the Knights Hospitallers (now the Knights of St. John), who founded it during the Middle Ages.

THE Natural History Museum of Ireland (next door to Leinster House) has the world's largest collection of insects.

THE River Farset, a tributary of the River Lagan, runs under High Street, Belfast, in a

The Albert Clock in Belfast is Ireland's leaning tower of Pisa. Built on swampland or 'sleech' in the 1860s, it is now four and a half feet off base.

The heights above Waterford City are known as Mount Misery.

tunnel that is big enough to accommodate a single decker bus.

WEST Belfast's grim 'Peace Line' is three times the height of the former Berlin Wall.

CARRIGAN Moss, which is gathered on beaches in Connemara, is valued worldwide as an aphrodisiac. Locals use it to cure sore throats.

TUMBLING 1800 feet off the Cock of Shruhill mountain in County Donegal, the Scardan Waterfall is the highest in Europe.

THE Ballymun flats on Dublin's northside were built in 1965 with money paid by the West German government as compensation for the 1941 air raid on Clontarf, which killed thirty-one people.

PHOENIX Park in Dublin covers 1800 acres. It is the largest city park in the world.

PROSPEROUS , County Kildare, was founded by one Robert Brooke, who went bankrupt twice, lost his family estate, and died in abject poverty.

THE Rotunda in Dublin, founded in 1745, was the first maternity hospital in Europe.

The 'Poisoned Glen' at the foot of Errigal
Mountain in County Donegal owes it name to the
former presence of the highly toxic Irish Spurge
Moss. The plant poisoned the drinking water, and
though the Spurge Moss is now extinct here,
farmers are still advised to keep their animals away
from the Glen's waters.

BELFAST has over twenty distinct dialects.

SKELLIG Michael off the coast of County Kerry marks the southernmost limit for arctic, and the northernmost limit for tropical fish.

FOUR hundred million tons of water rush through the narrows of Strangford Lough in County Down twice a day.

THE largest swimming pool in history was at Glenveagh House in County Donegal. In the 1930s, its millionaire Irish-American owner Henry P. McIlheny had the nearby lake centrally heated by steam pipes for visiting Hollywood glitterati.

UNDER the 1801 Copyright Act, Trinity College is entitled to one free copy of every book published annually in the British Isles. The university library now has over two million volumes and needs a quarter of a mile of new shelving every year.

SAINTS AND SCHOLARS

THE first Irish saint wasn't Patrick. It was St. Abban, who preached in southern England in the 2nd century.

SCOTLAND'S capital, Edinburgh, is named after the Irish nun Edana who founded a convent there in the 6th century.

JOSHUA Jacobs, leader of the weird 19th century White Quakers cult, once led his followers in naked procession through the streets of Dublin.

DESPITE its association with the national saint, Croagh Patrick in County Mayo has been a holy mountain since pagan times.

FLEET Street in London was the site of the city's first Irish community in the 6th century

In 1750, the Church of Ireland Bishop of Raphoe was shot dead while carrying out a highway robbery.

which was centred on a holy well dedicated to St. Brigid.

IRELAND'S holiest place is arguably the churchyard of St. Eanna on the Aran island of Inishmore. Over 120 recognised saints are buried there.

MOST of the famous *Book of Kells* was actually written in a monastery on the Scottish island of Iona.

THE Pope is also bishop of the tiny see of Kilfenora in County Clare.

THE sacred fire of St. Brigid, which was kept in an oak grove near Kildare, was extinguished by English soldiers in 1535, after supposedly burning continuously for nearly a thousand years.

IRELAND'S smallest church is at Portbraden in County Antrim. Only ten feet long by six feet wide, the structure is dedicated to St. Gobhnan – the patron saint of builders.

ST. Comgall of Bangor was said to possess miraculous spit which could shatter rocks.

THE soil on Devenish Island in County Fermanagh is reputed to have been brought

The Irish philosopher and scholar John Scotus
Eriugena met a rather bizarre end in 870 when he
was hacked to death with sharpened pens by
students he had forced to think.

According to the 12th century prophecies of St. Malachy, Ireland will be at peace when the shamrock meets the palm — in other words, when St. Patrick's Day falls on a Palm Sunday.

from the Colosseum in Rome in the 6th century by St. Molaise, because it was soaked with the blood of the early Christian martyrs.

AN obscure Protestant sect, the Dippers, baptize their members in the waters of Lough Erne which they believe to be the true River Jordan.

DISIBODE, an Irish saint of the 7th century, is credited with creating the German wine industry, when wines miraculously sprouted from a staff he had stuck into the soil along the banks of the Rhine.

A 'five o'clock shadow' can clearly be seen on the embalmed head of St. Oliver Plunkett, which is kept in St. Peter's Church, Drogheda, proving that he shaved on the morning of his execution in 1681.

KERRYMAN Monsignor Hugh O'Flaherty, 'the Scarlet Pimpernel of the Vatican', saved more than 14,000 Allied prisoners from the S.S. in occupied Rome between 1942–44.

EVERY March 6th, the Tricolour is flown from Swiss public buildings to celebrate the Irish saint, Fridolin.

AFTER their deaths, the scarlet hats of past

Primates of All Ireland are hung in the rafters of
Armagh Cathedral and left to rot as a symbol of
their owners' earthly mortality.

ICELAND was settled by Irish monks in the 8th
century.

ST. Kevin of Glendalough was an extreme
misogynist, who is said to have once hurled a
persistent female admirer to her death after she
had ventured into his mountain retreat.

IN the 7th century, St. Killian became the only
Irishman to be offered the Papacy. Amazingly,
he refused the honour.

IRELAND'S first lighthouse was built by monks
on Hook Head, County Wexford, in 810.

UNTIL the advent of steamships, it was
common practice for Irish sea captains to carry
pebbles from Scattery Island, home of the patron
saint of mariners, St. Cannera, in the belief that
they would prevent shipwreck.

MASS has been celebrated every Sunday at
Ballintobber Abbey in County Galway since
1216.

IRELAND'S only purpose-built mosque is in
Westport, County Mayo.

St. Fearghal declared that the world was round eight centuries before Galileo.

Beith, the grandson of Noah, is said to have landed
his ark, full of the world's most desirable females,
on Carnmore Point in County Fermanagh after
the great flood – hence the legendary beauty
of Irishwomen.

THE world's oldest New Testament, dating from the 2nd century, is in the Chester Beatty Library in Dublin.

THE village of Poyntzpass, County Down, on the fringes of Ulster's 'Bible Belt', has more churches per head of population than anywhere else in the world.

ST. Patrick is the patron saint of French fishermen.

ALTHOUGH there are over 1400 listed Irish saints only five have been officially canonized.

THE reformed Dublin alcoholic and would-be saint, Matt Talbot, who died in 1925, hung heavy iron chains around his body as a penance.

KING Henry V was cursed after letting his troops ransack the shrine of the Irishman St. Fiacre, the patron saint of haemorrhoid sufferers, at Meaux in France. Henry died as a result of his piles turning septic on August 30th 1417, the feastday of St. Fiacre.

THE Romans imported Irish wolfhounds, using them to devour Christians in the arena.

EERIE EIRE

DERMOT MacMurrough, who was responsible for bringing the Normans into Ireland, rotted to death for his sin in 1173, after contracting *morbis pediculosis*.

THE first mummy to be seen publicly outside Egypt was displayed in Belfast in 1824. It is still there.

IRELAND'S Atlantis, the legendary city of Hy Brasyl, is reputed to lie beneath the waters of Carlingford Lough.

THESPIAN suspicion over *Macbeth* – usually referred to as 'the Scottish play' – is thought to date from the time of the Irish actor-manager Spranger Barry (1719-1777), who was famous for his portrayal of the evil king. A life dogged by personal problems, law suits and agonising gout ended in poverty for the unfortunate Corkman.

The aristocratic Dublin rakes of the 18th century Hell Fire Club once set fire to a house and remained drinking inside it to get a foretaste of Hell itself.

Count Dracula was created by the
Dublin writer Bram Stoker.

UNTIL the 1920s, on St. Brigid's Day (February 1st) at Teltown, County Meath, couples could legally marry by simply walking towards each other. If the union didn't work out, they could 'divorce' by walking away from each other at the same place exactly a year and a day later.

JAMES Byrne, the 7 feet 2 inch 'Irish Giant', died of depression in 1783 after being literally watched to death by the servant of a doctor who wanted his huge frame for dissection.

THE Devil's Bit mountain near Thurles, County Tipperary, is so called because Satan, furious at finding no wicked souls in Ireland as he flew over it, supposedly bit a chunk out of the rock in his rage.

HALLOWEEN has its origins in Samhain, the Celtic feast of the dead.

A holy tree on the Tyrone shore of Lough Neagh near Ardboe was said to bring good fortune to those who hammered coins into its trunk. It eventually died of metal poisoning.

A monkey appears on the Fitzgerald coat of arms in tribute to the family pet which rescued the infant 1st Earl of Kildare from a fire at Kilkea castle in the 14th century.

IN 1991, English prophet and self-styled 'Son of God', David Icke, proclaimed that the Scottish island of Islay would sink into the sea because of 'bad vibes' emanating from the troubles in Ulster.

THE bullaun stone, which is kept in St. Matthew's Church on the Woodvale Road in Belfast, is said to have the power to cure warts, spots and acne.

A ship from Cobh discovered the ghostly wreck of the *Marie Celeste* in 1872.

THE crypt of St. Michan's Church in Dublin contains the almost perfectly preserved remains of corpses dating from the Middle Ages. The reason for their incorruption appears to be the limestone walls of their tombs.

ON the thirtieth anniversary of the Munich air disaster which wiped out the famous 'Busby Babes' football team, Manchester United played Coventry. The only goal of the game was scored by United's new Irish signing Liam O'Brien at 3.04 pm – the exact moment of impact three decades before.

ACCORDING to legend, the hair of anyone who swims in the lake on Slieve Gullion in County Armagh will turn grey overnight.

Supposedly transformed from fowl to fish by St. Patrick, the Lough Melvin trout tastes like roast chicken when cooked.

*The Electric Brae near Hilltown, County Down,
is the only place on Earth where water and other
objects appear to roll uphill, in defiance of the
law of gravity.*

THE folio number of the plans of the *Titanic*, built at the fiercely Protestant Belfast shipyard of Harland and Wolff, was 3909 04 which, when read backwards, is said to crudely spell 'NO POPE'.

FOR centuries, an unholy ringing sound coming from a gnarled old oak tree on windy nights terrified the people of the County Down village of Kilbroney. In 1885, the tree was blown down and the source of the ghostly noise was discovered – a golden bell hidden in the hollow of the trunk by a monk hundreds of years before.

ON 13th April 1829, the day that the United Kingdom Parliament gave the vote to Irish Catholics, the statue of George Walker – Protestant hero of the 1689 siege of Derry – which had stood quietly on the city's famous walls for more than a century, inexplicably crumbled.

THE first British soldier to die in the present troubles was Gunner Robert Curtis who was shot dead in Belfast in 1971. The IRA sniper who killed him was himself killed in a gun battle with the army the next day – in Curtis Street.

SQUIRE Watson, an eccentric 18th century

The medieval purgatory on Lough Derg, County Donegal, was believed to be one of the two entrances to Hell, Mount Etna on Sicily being the other.

Kilkenny landowner had such an unshakeable belief that he would be reincarnated as a fox that he had a luxurious marble den built in the grounds of his estate in anticipation of his return.

SINCE it opened in 1830, Dublin's Glasnevin Cemetery has been the last resting place for more than eleven million people.

IRELAND had its own werewolf legend. These creatures were believed to be the souls of the damned who had rejected the teachings of St. Patrick.

Arms and the Man

THE Dutch Blue Guards, the personal bodyguard of King William III, were devout Catholics to a man.

OVER 150,000 Irishmen fought in the American Civil War (1861-1865), accounting for one in sixteen of the combatants.

IN 1578, the Irish rebel James Fitzmaurice hired two thousand Italian mercenaries to help him free his homeland from the English. However, when the ships docked in Lisbon, his soldiers were commandeered by the King of Portugal. Every one of the would-be liberators of Ireland died in the trackless wastes of the Sahara.

THE commander of Drogheda, Sir Arthur Aston, was beaten to death with his own wooden leg after Cromwell's soldiers captured the town in 1649.

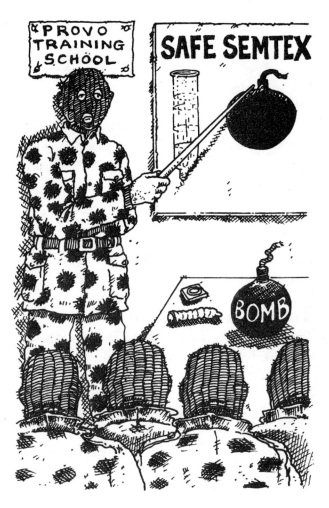

Condoms were an integral part of IRA bombs in the 1970s.

JOHN Barry of Wexford founded the U.S. Navy.

CHIEFTAINS in medieval Ulster went out of their way to marry Scotswomen because their dowries consisted of axe-wielding galloglass mercenaries. When Turlough Luineach O'Neill married Lady Agnes MacDonald of Kintyre in 1568, she brought 10,000 troops with her.

THE most one-sided battle in Irish history took place at Kinsale in 1601 when more than 2,000 Irishmen lost their lives compared with just one English fatality.

THE British Army base at Bessbrook, County Armagh, is the world's busiest heliport with some 200 flights daily to and from the Ulster border.

THE Bloody Oak, a tree standing near Armagh, contains fragments of bullets fired during the Battle of the Yellow Ford (a rare Irish victory), fought on the site in 1598.

LOUIS Brennan of Castlebar, County Mayo, invented the torpedo.

DUBLIN housewife Kit Welsh disguised herself as a man and served twenty years in the army of the Duke of Marlborough from 1692.

The Europa in Belfast city centre is the world's most bombed hotel, having been blasted thirty-three times since the first explosion in 1971.

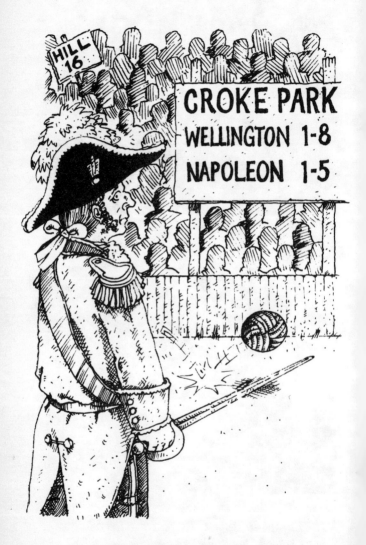

HILL 16

CROKE PARK
WELLINGTON 1-8
NAPOLEON 1-5

The Duke of Wellington was a Dubliner.

She was wounded four times without doctors discovering her secret and survived to be personally decorated for bravery by Queen Anne.

THE infamous Charge of the Light Brigade in 1854 was a direct result of the ineptitude of Mayoman Lord Bingham. Bingham was later promoted to the rank of field marshal.

BRUSSELS was liberated by the Irish Group of the British Army in 1944.

THE tough Mayo pirate queen Grace O'Malley once attacked a Turkish merchantman whilst heavily pregnant. Retiring below decks at the height of the ensuing sea battle, she is said to have given birth to a son before returning to sink the enemy ship and slaughter its crew.

THE Nazi broadcaster William Joyce, alias Lord Haw Haw, was from Salthill, County Galway.

THE main square of Buenos Aires, capital of Argentina, is called the Plaza Del Mayo in honour of Mayoman William Brown, founder of the country's navy.

CONCENTRATION camps were developed not by the Nazis, but by the Kerry-born British general Lord Kitchener during the Boer War (1899-1902).

KERRYMAN Dan O'Connell held the bizarre distinction of being both a French general and a British colonel at the same time during the Napoleonic Wars.

THE 1702 Battle of Cremona in northern Italy was fought entirely by Irishmen serving in the armies of Austria and France. Not surprisingly, the Irish won.

EAMONN de Valera shocked the world in 1945 when he called at the German embassy in Dublin to express his condolences on the death of Adolf Hitler.

THE famous phrase 'War is Hell' is attributed to the Cavan-born American Civil War general, Phil Sheridan.

ONE of the oddest military escapades in history took place in 1866 when Irish Fenians, veterans of the U.S. Civil War, invaded Canada with the intention of holding the entire country (all four million square miles of it) hostage in exchange for the freedom of Ireland.

THERE is a German military cemetery near Avoca, County Wicklow. It contains the

The only survivor, animal or human, of Custer's last stand in 1876 was Comanche, the horse of the Irish cavalry officer, Captain Myles Keogh.

*In 1922, at the height of the Civil War, Free State
brigadier Patrick Paul escaped from his Republican
captors in Waterford disguised as a
mother superior.*

remains of servicemen who crash-landed or whose bodies were washed up on the coast of Ireland during World War Two.

MEDIEVAL Irish soldiers decked and matted their hair as an effective protection against sword blows.

THOSE on the receiving end of 'the shots that echoed round the world' at Lexington in 1775 were soldiers of the Royal Irish Regiment.

THE modern submarine was invented by a Clare schoolteacher, John P. Holland. He was financed by the Fenian Brotherhood who intended to use it to sink Royal Navy ships.

AS a tribute to the city's role in the Battle of the Atlantic, the entire German U-boat fleet was surrendered to Derry before it was scuttled in 1945.

MORE than half of George Washington's army were of Irish extraction.

THE skull of Corkman, Sir Charles McCarthy, killed during a native revolt in 1824, is the most sacred relic of the Ashanti tribe of Ghana in West Africa.

SOME of the buildings on O'Connell Street in

During a particularly fierce siege in the 17th
century, the defenders of Moy Castle in County
Tyrone smeared the walls of their fortress with cow
dung to lessen the impact of enemy cannonballs.

Dublin still bear bullet holes dating from the 1916 Easter Rising.

THE phrase 'by hook or by crook' originated during Cromwell's 1649 campaign in Ireland when he vowed to capture Waterford by advancing by sea round Hook Head or through the village of Crooke.

THE first casualty of the Civil War (1922-23) was a Free State sniper smashed over the head with a teapot by an elderly Dublin woman.

OVER 400,000 Irishmen served France in the famous Irish Brigade between 1690 and 1792.

THE famous Irish general Owen Roe O'Neill, who never received so much as a scratch during a brilliant military career spanning thirty years, died of blood poisoning after stepping on a rusty nail in 1649.

Not a lot of people know that...

WILLIAM Hill, the founder of Britain's biggest bookmakers, served as a Black and Tan in Ireland.

IN 1986, a 900 year old cheese was found, perfectly preserved, in a Tipperary bog.

IRISH immigrant J. P. O'Malley died from electrocution after urinating onto the live rail of the New York subway system soon after it opened in 1904.

THE popularity of Patrick as a Christian name in Ireland is due to the great 17th century general, Patrick Sarsfield, not the national saint.

THE largest farm ever covered over four million acres (bigger than the whole of Northern Ireland) of Australia's Northern Territory, and was owned by Ulsterman Samuel McCaughey until his death in 1909.

One traditional Irish cure for a hangover was to be buried up to the neck in moist river sand.

LADY Castlereagh, wife of the famous 19th century Ulster diplomat Lord Castlereagh, reputedly had two snakes tattooed on the insides of her thighs.

THERE has been horse-racing at the Curragh since about the 1st century B.C.

IRELAND's premier peerage is the Earldom of Kinsale. The present incumbent is a Somerset plumber.

DURING his 1984 visit, President Ronald Reagan stopped off in a traditional Dublin pub. After taking one sip out of a pint of Guinness he left. His glass was then smashed by U.S. secret service agents.

THE *Turkish Delight* chocolate was first made in Cobh, County Cork, by the Hadji Bey company in the 1890s.

CLADDAGH rings originally signified that the marriage had been the result of an elopement.

THE Lough Erne Cot is the only boat in the world to be annually sunk. It is traditionally scuttled during the winter months in order to preserve the wood.

ANNE Boleyn was born in Ireland.

Good news for Belfastmen, they enjoy the best sex ratio in Ireland with some twelve women for every ten men. However, the boot is on the other foot in Counties Leitrim and Roscommon, where there are some ten women for every twelve men.

The phrase 'he digs with the other foot' to describe religious affiliation in Ulster dates from the 18th century when each district had its own spademaker. In Catholic areas, spades were generally designed to be used by the left foot, in Protestant areas to be used with the right.

MORE than 8,000,000 pints of Guinness are drunk every day in Ireland.

ANDREW Jackson is the only U.S. president not to have been born in America. He was born in the middle of the Atlantic in 1767 on an emigrant ship taking his parents from Carrickfergus.

THE Irish alphabet has only 18 letters: J, K, Q, V, W, X, Y and Z are all missing.

BELFAST'S bedevilment may stem from the fact that it is first mentioned by chroniclers in 666 A.D.

THE Burke family of Connacht claim direct descent from Charlemagne.

CAHIRCIVEEN in Kerry was once so inaccessible from the rest of Ireland that it was quicker to send newspapers and mail from Dublin via New York.

CEMENT was invented by Bryan Higgins of Sligo in 1779.

DOWNING Street in London is named after the 17th century Dublin-born politician, Sir Charles Downing.

ONE of the world's first women drivers was
Miss Jennie Richardson, who took the controls
of the Bessbrook to Newry tram in 1884.

DUBLIN is the only city in the world to have
produced three Nobel prizewinners for
Literature: W. B. Yeats (1923), George Bernard
Shaw (1925) and Samuel Beckett (1969).

THE legend of the Blarney Stone originated
when Cormac McCarthy found his stronghold at
Blarney, County Cork, surrounded by a hostile
English army. By deft use of flattery McCarthy
persuaded the English to raise their siege.

MAGILLIGAN Strand in County Derry was
the site of an unusual annual horse race in the
18th century. Church of Ireland clergymen
would race against their Presbyterian
counterparts with the winning side getting that
year's parish tithes.

THE ancestors of the first man on the moon,
Neil Armstrong, were from County Fermanagh.

FOSTERING was common in early medieval
Ireland.

THE only woman to become a Freemason was
Mary St. Leger of Mallow, Country Cork. She

Richard Martin, philanthropist and founder of the RSPCA, had a 30 mile long avenue leading up to the mansion on his 200,000 acre Galway estate.

The world's oddest royal family is that of the Caribbean island of Redonda. This crank dynasty was founded by an Irish sailor when his ship stopped off at this desolate rock in 1865. He passed the 'title' King of Redonda on to his descendants. The reigning monarch is a housewife in Manchester.

was enroled into the order in 1725 after secretly spying on a lodge meeting.

THE phrase 'the Emerald Isle' was first coined by the Belfast doctor and poet, William Drennan, in 1795.

ONE of the great gaffes in social history took place at Stormont in the 1920s. During an important function, Northern Ireland minister Dawson Bates – who was in attendance with his wife and son – entered the main hall. As the party made their way towards the gathered dignitaries, a flunky grandly announced 'the honourable Dawson Bates, his wife Lady Bates and their son Master Bates'.

TOM Gallagher of Derry invented the modern cigarette in 1888.

GLASGOW Celtic Football Club took both its name and its distinctive green and white hooped kit from Belfast Celtic, which folded in 1949.

THE last ever Great Auk was killed on the Saltee Islands off County Wexford by local fishermen in 1845.

GENERAL de Gaulle's maternal ancestors were McCartans from County Down.

THE original 'hole in the wall' bar was in 16th century Kilkenny.

FREDERICK Hervey, the eccentric 18th century Earl Bishop of Derry, used to sprinkle flour on the floor of his palace when he had guests staying. By following the footprints the following morning, he could find out who was sleeping with who.

IRELAND is the world's twentieth largest island.

THE first winner of the Victoria Cross, in 1854, was Charles Lucas of Clontibret, County Monaghan.

GUINNESS boss, the Earl of Iveagh (1847-1927), gave each of his three sons £5,000,000 in cash (over £100,000,000 in today's money) as a wedding present.

BELFAST inventor Joseph Black built a crude airship in the 1780s, shortly after the Montgolfier brothers launched the first hot air balloon in Paris.

THE greatest moment of Belfastman Steve Morrow's career came in 1993 when he scored the winning goal for Arsenal in the League Cup Final. His jubilant team mates hoisted him aloft

Pope Adrian IV offered the overlordship of Ireland to the English Crown in the bull Laudabiliter, *issued in 1155.*

Swallowing a live frog was a traditional Irish cure for stomach ache.

then almost immediately dropped him, breaking his arm.

SOME 60 million people outside Ireland claim Irish ancestry, including 44 million in the United States, eight million in Britain and three million in Australia.

DURING the years immediately after the Second World War, Dublin was the only major city in Europe in which meat was freely available.

DENNIS Kelly, racehorse owner and gambler extraordinaire, left a clause in his will that his heir should forfeit £400 for every bet he made.

KILKENNY'S long association with cats stems from the fearsome, wild felines which once inhabited the Dunmore caves in the north of the county.

HANDEL'S famous oratorio *The Messiah* received its world premiere in Fishamble Street in Dublin in 1742.

THE only Irish motor car manufacturers were Chambers Brothers of Belfast who turned out 500 hand-made models from their Newtownards Road factory between 1904 and 1927.

LORD Mayors of Limerick also hold the title 'Admirals of the Shannon'.

M.G.M.'s roaring lion was bred in Dublin Zoo.

THERE are no moles in Ireland.

THE fabled North West Passage was finally discovered by Wexfordman, Sir Robert McClure, in 1850.

MOLLY Malone actually existed. She died in 1734 and her headstone can be seen in Dublin's St. John's churchyard.

THE world's oldest daily newspaper is the *Belfast News Letter* which was founded in 1737.

THE Oscar statuette was designed by a Dublin-born art director, Cedric Gibbons. He went on to win nine.

THE first potatoes in Europe were planted by Sir Walter Raleigh in 1596 on his estate near Youghal, County Cork.

IRELAND formerly had five provinces: Connacht, Leinster, Munster, Ulster and Meath.

THE pneumatic tyre was invented in Belfast in

'Sweeney's Gun' is a complex of sea caves on
Lough Swilly. Every day, Atlantic rollers rushing
into the caverns create a bang so loud that in the
days before the motor car, the noise could
clearly be heard on the streets of Derry more
than thirty miles away.

The Department of Irish Folklore, University
College Dublin, has over 100,000 tales, myths and
legends on record, the largest collection of its kind
in the world.

1889 by the chemist, John Boyd Dunlop, for use on his young son's bicycle.

FROGS came to Ireland with the Normans.

IN 1770, the entire village of Rosapenna on Donegal's Inishowen Peninsula was buried overnight by a freak sandstorm.

DUBLIN is the oldest of all the Scandinavian-founded capitals, beating Reykjavik in Iceland by more than thirty years.

UNTIL the 9th century, the people of Ireland were known as Scots.

IN 1895 Irishman James Harden Hickey wrote a bestseller entitled *The Aesthetics of Suicide*, which listed 139 different ways of ending one's life. Three years later he killed himself.

FRESHLY gathered shamrock was once considered a delicacy in Ireland.

THE slate for the roof of the Houses of Parliament in London was taken from a now disused quarry on Kerry's Valentia Island.

THE tune of *The Star Spangled Banner*, the U.S. national anthem, was composed by the blind harper Carolan who died in 1738.

THE first steeplechase took place in County Cork in 1752 and was run between the spires of two churches near Mallow, hence the race's name.

SURNAMES were introduced to Ireland around the time of Brian Boru.

THE writer Jonathan Swift was so popular – or curmudgeonly – that he claimed an allowance of twenty shillings a year to replace hats worn out acknowledging people's greetings.

IRELAND once had its own version of the Olympics, the Tailteann Games, which were held on Lughnasa (August 1st), the feast of the Sun God.

THE Tricolour was first officially flown at the 1906 Athens Olympics on the insistence of Tipperary athlete, Peter O'Connor, who had just won the Gold medal for the Hop, Skip and Jump.

IN Germany, a Turkish Bath is known as an Irish Bath.

THE Union Jack was first raised not in England but over Dublin Castle on January 1st 1801.

The phrase 'to chance your arm' originated during the medieval feud between the Butler and Fitzgerald families. During one particularly fierce clash between the two sides in Dublin, fighting spilled into St. Patrick's Cathedral. With the battle going against him, the Earl of Ormonde, leader of the Butlers, barricaded himself in a room in the South Transept. Although offered terms by the Fitzgerald leader, the Earl of Kildare, the wary Ormonde refused to leave his sanctuary. To prove that his word was indeed his bond, Kildare hacked a hole in the door and stuck his arm through the opening, offering the hand of friendship to his enemy with no guarantee that it wouldn't be chopped off. The door, with its rough hewn hole, can still be seen.

An annual 12th of July march is held in Ghana, West Africa. The practice was introduced by Ulster missionaries in the 19th century. In Canada, a Mohawk Indian tribe has its own Orange lodge.

MR Valentine Valentine of Ballinamallard, County Fermamagh, celebrates his birthday on February 14th.

THE tune of *Waltzing Matilda*, unofficial anthem of Australia, was written by Robert Barton of Fermanagh.

IRELAND's last wolf was killed by huntsmen in County Carlow in 1786.

FERMANAGH M.P. 'silent' Frank Maguire never uttered a word during his six years in the House of Commons, yet he changed the course of British history in 1979, when his casting vote brought down Jim Callaghan's government, paving the way for Margaret Thatcher's sweep to power.